HOME

1894 - 1994

100 years in Cambridge

300 years in Education

1695 - 1995

Homerton College Centenary Anthology

Through the Windows of this Book

Poems about childhood
selected by tutors at Homerton College

edited by Morag Styles

designed and typeset by Alan Russell

printed by Soloprint, Eaton Socon, Cambs

Homerton College 1994

Preface

The idea for this book came at the end of a research seminar on poetry. It was a balmy, summer evening and we decided to move outside the Combination Room with our glasses of wine. It was Homerton at its best - relaxed people and lively debate in a pleasant setting. Someone suggested jokingly that an anthology of Homerton staff's favourite poems would be a good idea. I went home and thought, "Why not? It wouldn't take much work."

I was wrong about the work, but compiling this anthology has been a satisfying and enlightening experience. Tutors were asked to select one poem which was either a childhood favourite, or a poem about or for children. I realised that we would, regrettably, have to confine the book to teaching staff or the length would get out of hand. I then wrote to some retired tutors, many of whom contributed poems. Students with an artistic bent were invited to illustrate some of the poems. The result is a glorious miscellany: some of the best verse of the past, alongside contemporary poems and the oral tradition.

I hope these poetic evocations of childhood will give the reader as much pleasure as it has given me to edit this anthology celebrating one hundred years of Homerton College in Cambridge.

Morag Styles
March 1994

Kate Pretty

1991 -

BEFORE TEA

Emmeline
Has not been seen
For more than a week. She slipped between
The two tall trees at the end of the green . . .
We all went after her. *"Emmeline!"*

"Emmeline,
I didn't mean -
I only said that your hands weren't clean."
We went to the trees at the end of the green . . .
But Emmeline
Was not to be seen.

Emmeline
Came slipping between
The two tall trees at the end of the green.
We all ran up to her. "Emmeline!
Where have you been?
Where have you been?
Why, it's more than a week!" And Emmeline
Said, "Sillies, I went and saw the Queen.
She says my hands are *purfickly* clean!"

A.A. Milne

I loved its cadences as a child and the way in which Emmeline's absence for a week seemed so anarchic. Where had she been and how had she got away with it? I like too the way in which the poem manages to allude to a whole lost world of prescribed manners and childhood conflict over them.

Laurie Rousham

1990 -

DON'T PUT MUSTARD IN THE CUSTARD

DON'T

Don't do,
Don't do,
Don't do that.
Don't pull faces,
Don't tease the cat.

Don't pick your ears,
Don't be rude at school.
Who do they think I am?

Some kind of fool?

One day
they'll say
Don't put toffee in my coffee
don't pour gravy on the baby
don't put beer in his ear
don't stick your toes up his nose

Don't put confetti on the spaghetti
and don't squash peas on your knees.

Don't put ant in your pants
don't put mustard in the custard
don't chuck jelly at the telly
and don't throw fruit at the computer
don't throw fruit at the computer.

Don't what?
Don't throw fruit at the computer.
Don't what?
Don't throw fruit at the computer.
Who do they think I am?
Some kind of fool?

Michael Rosen

Don't Put Mustard in the Custard, the title poem from the above book, is my current favourite for reading to infants and has been for some years. One six-year old in a group that I read it to went on record as saying "It's better than Sonic the Hedgehog!"

David Whitley

1987 -

LICE-HUNTERS

When the kid's forehead is full of red torments
Imploring swarms of dreams with vague contents,
Two large and charming sisters come
With wafty fingers and silvery nails, to his bedroom.

They set the kid by a wide-open window where
A tangle of flowers bathes in the blue air
And run fine, alluring, terrible
Fingers through his thick dew-matted hair.

He hears the rustling of their timid breath
Flowered with the long pinkish vegetable honies underneath
Or broken anon, sibilant, the saliva's hiss
Drawn from a lip, or a desire to kiss.

He hears their black eyelashes beat in that quietude
and "Crack!" to break his inebriated indolences
Neath their electric and so soft fingers death assails
The little lice beneath their regal nails.

And Lo! there mounts within him Wine of Laziness - a squiffer's sigh
Might bring delirium - and the kid feels
Neath the slowness of their caresses, constantly
Wane and fade a desire to cry.

Ezra Pound

Why do some poems mean more to us than others? A rhythm to which we feel singularly attuned? A precise mixture of dreams and taut perceptions that seem to connect in deep ways with personal memories and make us able to see and feel more than we thought possible? Lice-Hunters has done all this for me.

Sheila Miles

1988 -

A PIPER

A piper in the streets today
Set up, and tuned, and started to play,
And away, away, away on the tide
Of his music we started; on every side
Doors and windows were opened wide,
And men left down their work and came,
And women with petticoats coloured like flame.
And little bare feet that were blue with cold,
Went dancing back to the age of gold,
And all the world went gay, went gay,
For half an hour in the street today.

Seumas O'Sullivan

I remember this from my primary school and used to dance my way home saying it to myself, pigtails flying.

David Whitebread

1986 -

HEADMASTER'S HYMN
(to be sung)

When a knight won his spurs
In the stories of old,
He was - *'Face the front, David Briggs,*
What have you been told?'
With a shield on his arm
And a lance in his - *'Hey!*
Is that a ball I can see?
Put - it - a - way.'

No charger have I
And - *'No talking back there.*
You're supposed to be singing,
Not combing your hair.'
Though back into storyland
Giants have - *'Roy,*
This isn't the playground,
Stop pushing that boy!'

Let faith be my shield
And - *'Who's eating sweets here?*
I'm ashamed of you, Marion,
It's not like you dear.'
And let me set free
With - *'Please stop that, Paul King.*
This is no place for whistlers,
We'd rather you sing!'

Allan Ahlberg

I chose this poem because it reminds me so wonderfully of myself, as a Deputy Headteacher, taking Hymn Practice every Thursday morning for the last three and a half years of my teaching career. This is actually my all time favourite hymn and I have, happily, very fond memories of 200 or so shining, wonderful young folk belting this out with all the glee they could muster. We always used to 'raise the roof' with this one!

Barry Jones

1971

PAGE D'ÉCRITURE

Deux et deux quatre
quatre et quatre huit
huit et huit font seize...
Répétez! dit le maître
Deux et deux quatre
quatre et quatre huit
huit et huit font seize.
Mais voilà l'oiseau-lyre
qui passe dans le ciel
l'enfant le voit
l'enfant l'entend
l'enfant l'appelle :
Sauve-moi
joue avec moi
oiseau!
Alors l'oiseau descend
et joue avec l'enfant
Deux et deux quatre...
Répétez! dit la maître
et l'enfant joue
l'oiseau joue avec lui...
Quatre et quatre huit
huit et huit font seize
et seize et seize qu'est-ce qu'ils font?
Ils ne font rien seize et seize
et surtout pas trente-deux
de toute façon
et ils s'en vont.
Et l'enfant a caché l'oiseau
dans son pupitre
et tous les enfants
entendent sa chanson
et tous les enfants
entendent la musique
et huit et huit à leur tour s'en vont
et quatre et quatre et deux et deux
à leur tour fichent le camp
et un et un ne font ni une ni deux
un à un s'en vont également.
Et l'oiseau-lyre joue
et l'enfant chante
et le professeur crie :
Quand vous aurez fini de faire le pitre!
Mais tous les autres enfants
écoutent la musique
et les murs de la classe
s'éroulent tranquillement.
Et les vitres redeviennent sable
l'encre redevient eau
les pupitres redeviennent arbres
la craie redevient falaise
le porte-plume redevient oiseau.

Jacques Prévert

Maths was not one of my better subjects in school, so when I first read this Prévert poem I felt he really portrayed my own feelings towards maths lessons and the strange expression "8 and 8 MAKE 16". "Making" was something I never did in maths! When I came to Homerton and "taught" Prévert, the poem took on another meaning; more of "les enfants qui chantent" and less of "le professeur qui crie..."

Libby Jared

1988 -

MATILDA

who told lies, and was burned to death

Matilda told such Dreadful Lies'
It made one Gasp and Stretch one's Eyes;
Her Aunt, who from her Earliest Youth,
Had kept a Strict Regard for Truth,
Attempted to Believe Matilda:
The effort very nearly killed her,
And would have done so, had not She
Discovered this Infirmity.
For once, towards the Close of Day,
Matilda, growing tired of play,
And finding she was left alone,
Went tiptoe to the Telephone
And summoned the Immediate Aid
Of London's Noble Fire-Brigade.
Within an hour the Gallant Band
Were pouring in on every hand,
From Putney, Hackney Downs and Bow.
With Courage high and Hearts a-glow,
They galloped, roaring through the Town,
'Matilda's House is Burning Down!'
Inspired by British Cheers and Loud
Proceeding from the Frenzied Crowd,
They ran their ladders through a score
Of windows on the Ball Room Floor;
And took Peculiar Pains to Souse
The Pictures up and down the House,
Until Matilda's Aunt succeeded
In showing them they were not needed;
And even then she had to pay
To get the Men to go away!

It happened that a few Weeks later
Her Aunt was off to the Theatre
To see that Interesting Play
The Second Mrs Tanqueray.
She had refused to take her Niece
To hear that Entertaining Piece:
A Deprivation Just and Wise
To Punish her for Telling Lies.
That Night a Fire DID break out-
You should have heard Matilda Shout!
You should have heard her Scream and Bawl,
And throw the window up and call
To People passing in the Street-
(The rapidly increasing Heat
Encouraging her to obtain
Their confidence) - but all in vain!
For every time She shouted 'Fire!'
They only answered 'Little Liar!'
And therefore when her Aunt returned,
Matilda, and the House, were Burned.

Hilaire Belloc

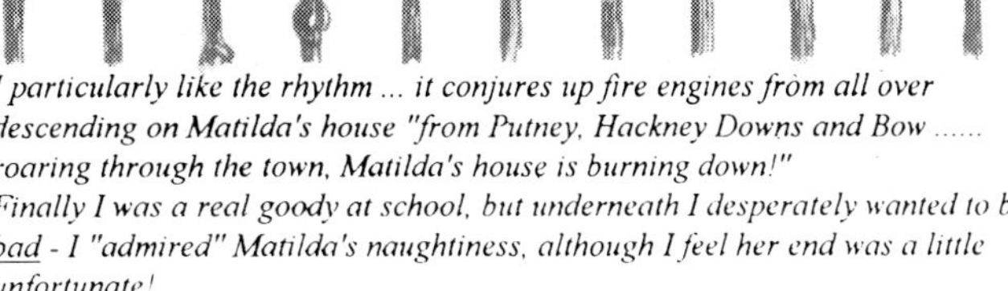

I particularly like the rhythm ... it conjures up fire engines from all over descending on Matilda's house "from Putney, Hackney Downs and Bow ...... roaring through the town, Matilda's house is burning down!"
Finally I was a real goody at school, but underneath I desperately wanted to be _bad_ *- I "admired" Matilda's naughtiness, although I feel her end was a little unfortunate!*

Peter Raby

1973 -

SCHOOL AT FOUR O'CLOCK

At four o'clock the building enters harbour.
All day it seems that we have been at sea.
Now, having lurched through the last of the water,
We lie, stone-safe, beside the jumping quay.
The stiff waves propped against the classroom window,
The razor-back of cliffs we never pass,
The question-mark of green coiling behind us,
Have all turned into cabbages, slates, grass.

Up the slow hill a squabble of children wanders
As silence dries the valley like a drought,
When suddenly that speechless cry is raging
Once more round these four walls to be let out.
Like playing cards the Delabole slates flutter,
The founding stone is shaken in its mine,
The faultless evening light begins to stutter
As the cry hurtles down the chimney-spine.

Packing my bag with useless bits of paper
I wonder, when the last word has been said,
If I'd prefer to find each sound was thudding
Not round the school, but just inside my head.
I watch where the street lamp with sodium finger
Touches the darkening voices as they fall.
Outside? Inside? Perhaps either condition's
Better than his who hears nothing at all.

And I recall another voice. A teacher
Long years ago, saying, *I think I know*
Where all the children come from, but the puzzle
To me is, as they grow up, where they go?
Love, wonder, marvellous hope. All these can wither
With crawling years like flowers on a stalk;
Or, to some Piper's tune, vanish for ever
As creatures murdered on a morning walk.

Though men may blow this building up with powder,
Drag its stone guts to knacker's yard, or tip,
Smash its huge heart to dust, and spread the shingle
By the strong sea, or sink it like a ship -
Listen. Through the clear shell of air the voices
Still strike like water from the mountain bed;
The cry of those who to a certain valley
Hungry and innocent came. And were not fed.

Charles Causley.

I love this poem for its unexpected rhythms and images, and the almost painful lucidity. It expresses for me something of the mystery of childhood, and a sense of the wonder which should be everyone's right, and too often isn't.

Tony Crowe

1963 - 1993

A CHILD'S HEAD

In it there is a space-ship
and a project
for doing away with piano lessons.

And there is
Noah's ark,
which shall be first.

And there is
an entirely new bird,
an entirely new hare,
an entirely new bumble-bee.

There is a river
that flows upwards.

There is a multiplication table.

There is anti-matter.

And it just cannot be trimmed.

I believe
that only what cannot be trimmed
is a head.

There is much promise
in the circumstance
that so many people have heads.

Miroslav Holub

I have long liked this poem because of its expression of the child's creative imagination, the poetic spirit that is in all of us, and for its wonderful last three lines. Recently I worked on it with a Parkside class to make an animation from and was fortunate in recording the poet reading it when he came to Cambridge. He didn't seem to mind our changing his title from "A Boy's Head", but did say he wrote it for his son when the boy was about ten years of age.

Liz Edwards

1984 - 1993

JABBERWOCKY

'Twas brillig, and the slithy toves
Did gyre and gimble in the wabe:
All mimsy were the borogoves,
And the mome raths outgrabe.

"Beware the Jabberwock, my son!
The jaws that bite, the claws that catch!
Beware the Jubjub bird, and shun
The frumious Bandersnatch!"

He took his vorpal sword in hand:
Long time the manxome foe he sought -
So rested he by the Tumtum tree,
And stood awhile in thought.

And, as in uffish thought he stood,
The Jabberwock, with eyes of flame,
Came whiffling through the tulgey wood,
And burbled as it came!

One, two! One, two! And through and through
The vorpal blade went snicker-snack!
He left it dead, and with its head
He went galumphing back.

"And, hast thou slain the Jabberwock?
Come to my arms, my beamish boy!
O frabjous day! Callooh! Callay!"
He chortled in his joy.

'Twas brillig, and the slithy toves
Did gyre and gimble in the wabe:
All mimsy were the borogoves,
And the mome raths outgrabe.

Lewis Carroll.

This is the first poem I remember learning by heart and reciting. I just loved the words and the whole surreal drama of the poem. I remember wishing the words were "real" words.

Helen Nicholson

1992 -

FAFNIR

In the quiet waters
Of the forest pool
Fafnir the dragon
His tongue will cool

His tongue will cool
And his muzzle dip
Until the soft waters lave
His muzzle-tip

Happy the dragon
In the days expended
Before the time had come for dragons
To be hounded

Delivered in their simplicity
To the Knights of the Advancing Band
Who seeing the simple dragon
Must kill him out of hand.

When thy body shall be torn
And thy lofty spirit
Broken into pieces
For a Knight's merit,

When thy life-blood shall be spilt
And thy Being mild
In torment and dismay
To Death beguiled

Fafnir, I shall say then,
Thou art better dead
For the Knights have burnt thy grass
And thou couldst not have fed.

The time has come yet
But must come soon
Meanwhile happy Fafnir
Take thy rest in the afternoon.

Take thy rest
Fafnir while thou mayest
In the long grass
Where thou liest

Happy knowing not
In thy simplicity
That the Knights have come
To do away with thee.

Stevie Smith

This is a wonderful poem to read aloud; it has a peculiarly hypnotic quality which belies the seriousness of the theme. I first learnt it as a twelve year old, when I saw the poem as an awful warning about the future and I liked that sense of saying something important out loud.

Janet Bottoms

1990 -

from THE FORSAKEN MERMAN

Come, dear children, let us away;
Down and away below!
Now my brothers call from the bay,
Now the great winds shoreward blow,
Now the salt tides seaward flow;
Now the wild white horses play,
Champ and chafe and toss in the spray.
Children dear, let us away!
This way, this way!

Call her once before you go -
Call once yet!
In a voice that she will know:
"Margaret! Margaret!"
Children's voices should be dear
(Call once more) to a mother's ear;
Children's voices, wild with pain -
Surely she will come again!
Call her once and come away;
This way, this way!
"Mother dear, we cannot stay!
The wild white horses foam and fret."
Margaret! Margaret!

Come, dear children, come away down;
Call no more!
One last look at the white-walled town,
And the little gray church on the windy
shore,
The come down!
She will not come though you call all day;
Come away, come away!

Children dear, was it yesterday
We heard the sweet bells over the bay?
In the caverns where we lay,
Through the surf and through the swell,
The far-off sound of a silver bell?
Sand-strewn caverns, cool and deep,
Where the winds are all asleep;
Where the spent lights quiver and gleam,
Where the salt weed sways in the stream,
Where the sea beasts, ranged all round,
Feed in the ooze of their pasture ground;
Where the sea snakes coil and twine,
Dry their mail and bask in the brine;
Where great whales come sailing by,
Sail and sail, with unshut eye,
Round the world for ever and aye?
When did music come this way?
Children dear, was it yesterday?

_ _ _ _ _ _ _ _ _ _ _ _

But, children, at midnight,
When soft the winds blow,
When clear falls the moonlight,
When spring tides are low;
When sweet airs come seaward
From heaths starred with broom,
And high rocks throw mildly
On the blanched sands a gloom;
Up the still, glistening beaches,
Up the creek we will hie,
Over banks of bright seaweed
The ebb-tide leaves dry.
We will gaze, from the sand-hills,
At the white, sleeping town;
At the church on the hillside -
And then come back down.
Singing: "There dwells a loved one,
But cruel is she!
She left lonely forever
The kings of the sea."

Matthew Arnold.

I don't know that a short extract can really do justice to what I responded to in this poem as a child, so I have quoted most of the poem. I enjoyed the aural and visual images combined with the sense of something rich and strange and yet recognisable in human terms, perhaps. I probably just revelled in melancholy.

Jenny Daniels

1988 -

CARGOES

QUINQUIREME of Nineveh from distant Ophir
Rowing home to haven in sunny Palestine,
With a cargo of ivory
And apes and peacocks,
Sandalwood, cedarwood, and sweet white wine.

Stately Spanish galleon coming from the Isthmus,
Dipping through the Tropics by the palm-green shores,
With a cargo of diamonds,
Emeralds, amethysts,
Topazes, and cinnamon, and gold moidores.

Dirty British coaster with a salt-caked smoke stack
Butting through the Channel in the mad March days,
With a cargo of Tyne coal,
Road-rail, pig-lead,
Firewood, ironware, and cheap tin trays.

John Masefield

I grew up in an isolated moorland village and poetry for me was largely playground chants or hymns. I remember clearly the day we learnt 'Cargoes' in primary school. I think I knew about 'cheap tin trays', but the rest of the poem was so exotic! I think I felt, rather than knew, after reading this, just how exciting and bursting with possibilities language could be. It also sounds so wonderful.

Sylvia Williams

1964 -

MARKET SQUARE

I had a penny,
A bright new penny,
I took my penny
  To the market square.
I wanted a rabbit,
A little brown rabbit,
And I looked for a rabbit
'Most everywhere.

For I went to the stall where they sold sweet lavender
("Only a penny for a bunch of lavender!").
"Have you got a rabbit, 'cos I don't want lavender?"
    But they hadn't got a rabbit, not anywhere there.

I had a penny,
And I had another penny,
I took my pennies
  To the market square.
I did want a rabbit,
A little baby rabbit,
And I looked for rabbits
  'Most everywhere.

And I went to the stall where they sold fresh mackerel
("Now then! Tuppence for a fresh-caught mackerel!").
"Have you got a rabbit, 'cos I don't like mackerel?"
  But they hadn't got a rabbit, not anywhere there.

I found a sixpence,
A little white sixpence.
I took it in my hand
    To the market square.
I was buying my rabbit
(I do like rabbits),
And I looked for my rabbit
    'Most everywhere.

So I went to the stall where they sold fine saucepans
("Walk up, walk up, sixpence for a saucepan!").
"Could I have a rabbit, 'cos we've got two saucepans?"
    But they hadn't got a rabbit, not anywhere there.

I had nuffin',
No, I hadn't got nuffin',
So I didn't go down
    To the market square;
But I walked on the common
The old-gold common . . .
And I saw little rabbits
    'Most everywhere!

So I'm sorry for the people who sell fine saucepans,
I'm sorry for the people who sell fresh mackerel,
I'm sorry for the people who sell sweet lavender,
    'Cos they haven't got a rabbit, not anywhere there!

A.A. Milne.

I only became really interested in poems when I had my own kids. As I read this it reminded me of my childhood in the war - going to market with my mother to queue for rabbits - a real find in a time of little food.

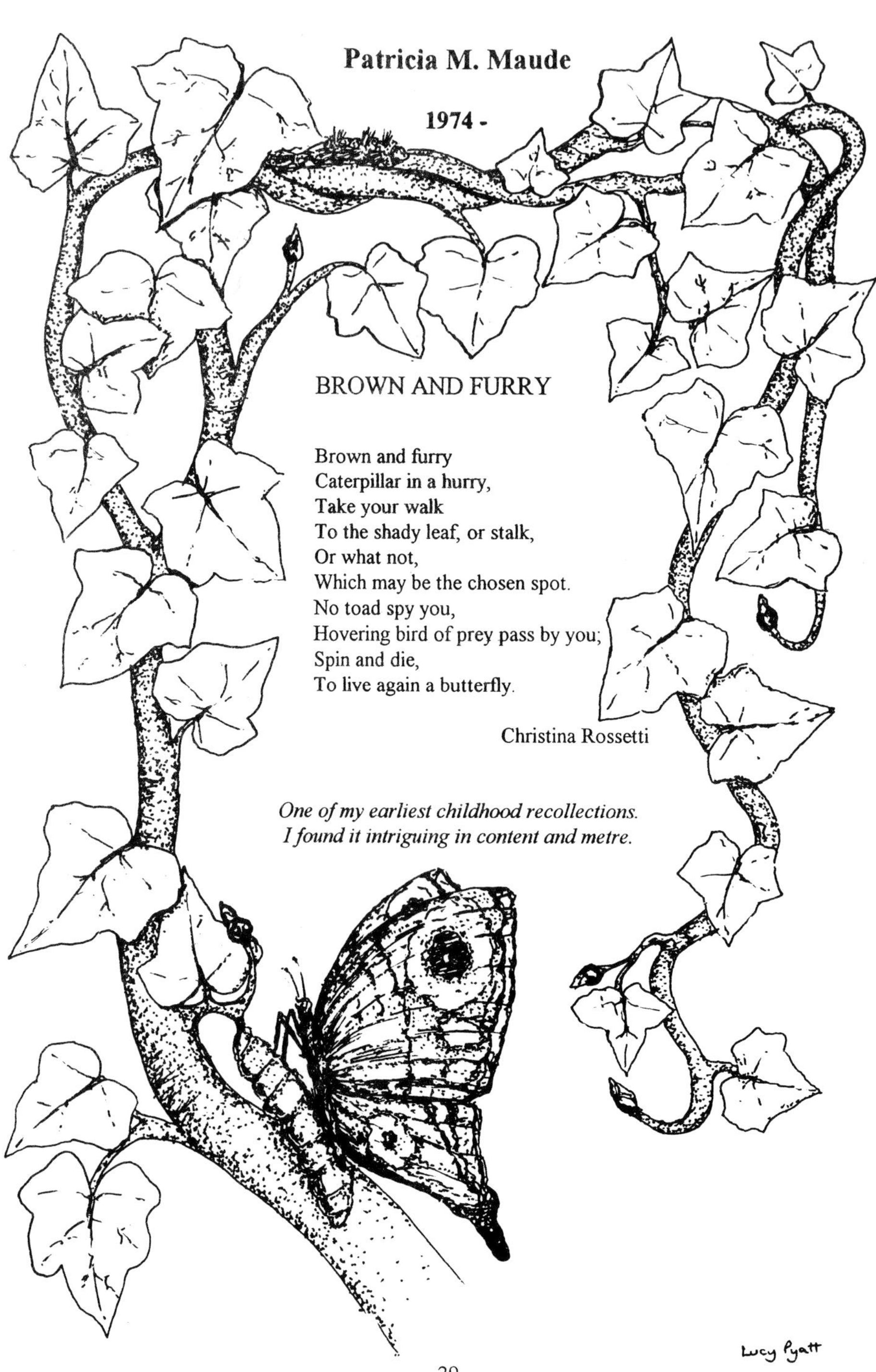

Patricia M. Maude

1974 -

BROWN AND FURRY

Brown and furry
Caterpillar in a hurry,
Take your walk
To the shady leaf, or stalk,
Or what not,
Which may be the chosen spot.
No toad spy you,
Hovering bird of prey pass by you;
Spin and die,
To live again a butterfly.

Christina Rossetti

One of my earliest childhood recollections.
I found it intriguing in content and metre.

Lucy Pyatt

Frances Weddell

1966 - 1987

THE FROG

What a wonderful bird the frog are -
When he sit, he stand almost;
When he hop, he fly almost.
He ain't got no sense hardly;
He ain't got no tail hardly either.
When he sit, he sit on what he ain't got - almost.

Anon

I've always liked this poem, doubtless by an ESL enjoyer of English!

George Hubbard

1976 - 1993

CHILDREN, behold the Chimpanzee:
He sits on the ancestral tree
From which we sprang in ages gone.
I'm glad we sprang: had we held on,
We might, for aught that I can say,
Be horrid Chimpanzees to-day.

Oliver Herford

*It's an interesting reflection on Darwin's theory of evolution ..
and it makes me laugh!*

Alison Wood

1968 -

THE THREE FOXES

Once upon a time there were three little foxes
Who didn't wear stockings, and they didn't wear sockses,
But they all had handkerchiefs to blow their noses,
And they kept their handkerchiefs in cardboard boxes.

They lived in the forest in three little houses,
And they didn't wear coats, and they didn't wear trousies.
They ran through the woods on their little bare tootsies,
And they played "Touch last" with a family of mouses.

They didn't go shopping in the High Street shopses,
But caught what they wanted in the woods and copses.
They all went fishing, and they caught three wormses,
They went out hunting, and they caught three wopses.

They went to a Fair, and they all won prizes -
Three plum-puddingses and three mince-pieses.
They rode on elephants and swang on swingses,
And hit three coco-nuts at coco-nut shieses.

That's all that I know of the three little foxes
Who kept their handkerchiefs in cardboard boxes.
They lived in the forest in three little houses,
But they didn't wear coats and they didn't wear trousies,
And they didn't wear stockings and they didn't wear sockses.

A.A. Milne.

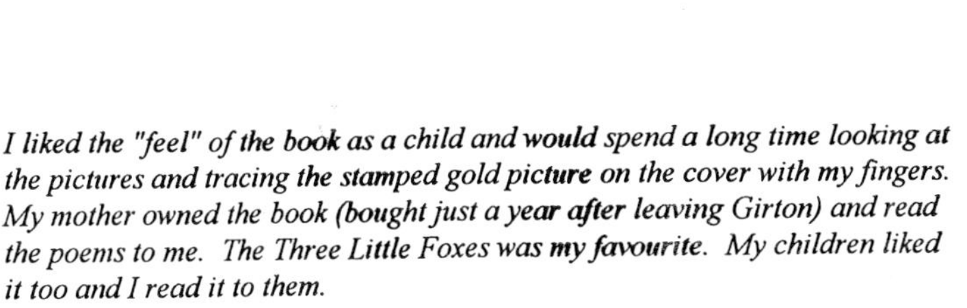

I liked the "feel" of the book as a child and would spend a long time looking at the pictures and tracing the stamped gold picture on the cover with my fingers. My mother owned the book (bought just a year after leaving Girton) and read the poems to me. The Three Little Foxes was my favourite. My children liked it too and I read it to them.

Harriet Allen

1986 -

from SKIMBLESHANKS: THE RAILWAY CAT

He will watch you without winking and he sees what you are
thinking
And it's certain that he doesn't approve
Of hilarity and riot, so the folk are very quiet
When Skimble is about and on the move.
You can play no pranks with Skimbleshanks!
He's a Cat that cannot be ignored;
So nothing goes wrong on the Northern Mail
When Skimbleshanks is aboard.

T.S. Eliot

When I was born, my family had a cat called Bill Bear. Apparently he walked out soon after and went to live with the local dentist. He would come back and sit in the garden, but could never be enticed back inside. I grew up with this story of a jealous cat, as an illustration of the fickle nature of these animals. I used to wonder at his name but was told that 'the naming of cats is a difficult matter...' At about the age of nine I was given "Old Possum's Book of Practical Cats" and Skimbleshanks soon became a favourite for its rhyme and rhythm.

Elizabeth Cook

1958 - 1983

ON A CAT AGEING

He blinks upon the hearth-rug
And yawns in deep content,
Accepting all the comforts
That Providence has sent.

Louder he purrs, and louder,
In one glad hymn of praise
For all the night's adventures,
For quiet, restful days.

Life will go on for ever,
With all that cat can wish:
Warmth and the glad procession
Of fish and milk and fish.

Only - the thought disturbs him -
He's noticed once or twice,
The times are somehow breeding
A nimbler race of mice.

Alexander Gray

Watching successive generations of my own cats has prepared me to notice in myself the phenomenon imaged in this poem. As a child brought up in the lap of the English Church I liked its modulated echoes of the sentiments and rhythms of Anglican hymnody. Children of a different background still seem to like its dry humour.

Anne Thwaites

1976 -

THE OWL AND THE PUSSY-CAT

The Owl and the Pussy-Cat went to sea
In a beautiful pea-green boat,
They took some honey, and plenty of money,
Wrapped up in a five-pound note.
The Owl looked up to the stars above,
And sang to a small guitar,
"O lovely Pussy! O Pussy, my love,
What a beautiful Pussy you are,
You are,
You are!
What a beautiful Pussy you are!"

Pussy said to the Owl, "You elegant fowl!
How charmingly sweet you sing!
O let us be married! too long we have tarried:
But what shall we do for a ring?"
They sailed away for a year and a day,
To the land where the Bong-tree grows,
And there in a wood a Piggy-wig stood,
With a ring at the end of his nose,
His nose,
His nose,
With a ring at the end of his nose.

"Dear Pig, are you willing to sell for one shilling
Your ring?" Said the Piggy, "I will."
So they took it away, and were married next day
By the Turkey who lives on the hill.
They dined on mince, and slices of quince,
Which they ate with a runcible spoon;
And hand in hand, on the edge of the sand,
They danced by the light of the moon,
The moon,
The moon,
They danced by the light of the moon.

Edward Lear

Firstly, I remember being part of a primary school performance of the poem which took place on a 'proper' stage at King Alfred's College, Winchester - I don't remember my part...! Secondly, my younger son loved the Picture Lion edition and at a young age delighted grand-parents by reciting it.

Rachel Sparks

1989 -

extract from
THE SONG OF HIAWATHA

Then the little Hiawatha
Learned of every bird its language,
Learned their names and all their secrets
How they built their nests in summer
Where they hid themselves in winter
Talked with them when'er he met them,
Called them 'Hiawatha's chickens'.

Henry Wadsworth Longfellow

As an infant the verse from 'Hiawatha' was the first 'proper poem' I ever memorised. I liked the rhythm and reciting it with the rest of my class. I spent a lot of time wondering what a 'Watha' was and how someone who was 'higher' could also be little.

Julia Anghileri

1989 -

ROGER THE DOG

Asleep he wheezes at his ease.
He only wakes to scratch his fleas.

He hogs the fire, he bakes his head
As if it were a loaf of bread.

He's just a sack of snoring dog,
You can lug him like a log.

You can roll him with your foot,
He'll stay snoring where he's put.

I take him out for exercise,
He rolls in cowclap up to his eyes.

He will not race, he will not romp,
He saves his strength for gobble and chomp.

He'll work as hard as you could wish
Emptying his dinner dish,

Then flops flat, and digs down deep,
Like a miner, into sleep.

Ted Hughes

..... for all the pleasure it has given my children.

Peter Cunningham

1990 -

THE RESCUE

The wind is loud,
The wind is blowing,
The waves are big,
The waves are growing.
What's that? What's that?
A dog is crying,
It's in the sea,
A dog is crying.
His or hers
Or yours or mine?
A dog is crying,
A dog is crying.

Is no one there?
A boat is going,
The waves are big,
A man is rowing,
The waves are big,
The waves are growing.
Where's the dog?
It isn't crying.
His or hers
Or yours or mine?
Is it dying?
Is it dying?

The wind is loud,
The wind is blowing,
The waves are big,
The waves are growing.
Where's the boat?
It's upside down.
And where's the dog,
And must it drown?
His or hers
Or yours or mine?
O, must it drown?
O, must it drown?

Where's the man?
He's on the sand,
So tired and wet
He cannot stand.
And where's the dog?
It's in his hand,
He lays it down
Upon the sand.
His or hers
Or yours or mine?
The dog is mine,
The dog is mine!

So tired and wet
And still it lies.
I stroke its head,
It opens its eyes,
It wags its tail,
So tired and wet.
I call its name,
For it's my pet,
Not his or hers
Or yours, but mine -
And up it gets,
And up it gets!

Ian Serraillier.

Because it's musical, pictorial, vocative, narrative, suspenseful; because big juniors and little infants all enjoy it; because it made me cry when I read it aloud and the children didn't seem to mind.

Ian Morrison

1970 -

SEA FEVER

I must go down to the seas again, to the lonely sea and the
sky,
And all I ask is a tall ship and a star to steer her by,
And the wheel's kick and the wind's song and the white
sail's shaking,
And a grey mist on the sea's face, and a grey dawn breaking.

I must go down to the seas again, for the call of the
running tide
Is a wild call and a clear call that may not be denied;
And all I ask is a windy day with the white clouds flying,
And the flung spray and the brown spume, and the sea-
gulls crying.

I must go down to the seas again, to the vagrant gypsy life,
To the gull's way and the whale's way where the wind's like
a whetted knife;
And all I ask is a merry yarn from a laughing fellow-rover,
And quiet sleep and a sweet dream when the long trick's
over.

John Masefield

I grew up on the north coast of Northern Ireland. Memories of childhood include gales and mountainous sea, and the small coasters riding out in the bay waiting for high tide to enter the river and go inland to the harbour at Coleraine. The Headteacher of Portstewart Primary School tried to introduce poetry to us by scenes we recognised. Sadly he did not always succeed.

Stephen Tomkins

1992 -

maggie and milly and molly and may
went down to the beach (to play one day)

and maggie discovered a shell that sang
so sweetly she couldn't remember her troubles, and

milly befriended a stranded star
whose rays five languid fingers were:

and molly was chased by a horrible thing
which raced sideways while blowing bubbles: and

may came home with a smooth round stone
as small as a world and as large as alone.

For whatever we lose (like a you or a me)
it's always ourselves we find in the sea

E.E. Cummings

None of us are anything without our interaction with the environment. The natural world provides us with joy, fascination, a justified caution and a deep wonder at our own existence. This poem also encapsulates for me, so much of children's vitality and freshness to situations. Observing children like these is one of the greatest rewards that teachers have in their own lives. It's a fine little poem.

PeterWarner

1980 -

from THE BOROUGH

Now is it pleasant in the summer-eve,
When a broad shore retiring waters leave,
Awhile to wait upon the firm fair sand,
When all is calm at sea, all still at land;
And there the ocean's produce to explore,
As floating by, or rolling on the shore;
Those living jellies which the flesh inflame,
Fierce as a nettle, and from that its name;
Some in huge masses, some that you may bring
In the small compass of a lady's ring;
Figured by hand divine - there's not a gem
Wrought by man's art to be compared to them;
Soft, brilliant, tender, through the wave they glow,
And make the moonbeam brighter where they flow.
Involved in sea-wrack, here you find a race,
Which science doubting, knows not where to place;
On shell or stone is dropp'd the embryo-seed,
And quickly vegetates a vital breed.

While thus with pleasing wonder you inspect
Treasures the vulgar in their scorn reject,
See as they float along th'entangled weeds
Slowly approach, upborne on bladdery beads;
Wait till they land, and you shall then behold
The fiery sparks those tangled fronds infold,
Myriads of living points; th'unaided eye
Can but the fire and not the form descry.
And now your view upon the ocean turn,
And there the splendour of the waves discern;
Cast but a stone, or strike them with an oar,
And you shall flames within the deep explore;
Or scoop the stream phosphoric as you stand,
And the cold flames shall flash along your hand;
When, lost in wonder, you shall walk and gaze
On weeds that sparkle, and on waves that blaze.

George Crabbe

Crabbe is an easy choice for me as most of my childhood was spent close to the Suffolk coast, not far from Aldeburgh, which is the subject of this poem. Some things never change; this vivid description of jellyfish along the seashore could have been written yesterday. Crabbe wrote it sometime before 1810 in comparative old age, yet it captures the vision and wonder of childhood. The seaside is one of the most formative experiences for children lucky enough to be taken there; who can forget the horror and fascination, or indeed the pain, of that first encounter with a jellyfish? For children the seaside is a place of discovery where the mysteries of the deep are cast up for inspection. Several of Crabbe's poems from this period reflect on visions of the night-time. His wife, Sarah, was mentally disturbed and afraid to leave the house or to be left on her own, so that during the day Crabbe was a virtual prisoner in his own home. Perhaps, when Sarah was asleep at night, he wandered along the phosphorescent shore, reflecting on his own childhood to escape his unhappiness, and indulging his passion for natural history and science. Here, with him, 'lost in wonder, you shall walk and gaze on weeds that sparkle, and on waves that blaze.'

Susan Macklin

1972 - 1993

THE WILD SWANS AT COOLE

The trees are in their autumn beauty,
The woodland paths are dry,
Under the October twilight the water
Mirrors a still sky;
Upon the brimming water among the stones
Are nine-and-fifty swans.

The nineteenth autumn has come upon me
Since I first made my count;
I saw, before I had well finished,
All suddenly mount
And scatter wheeling in great broken rings
Upon their clamorous wings.

I have looked upon those brilliant creatures,
And now my heart is sore.
All's changed since I, hearing at twilight,
The first time on this shore,
The bell-beat of their wings above my head,
Trod with a lighter tread.

Unwearied still, lover by lover,
They paddle in the cold
Companionable streams or climb the air;
Their hearts have not grown old;
Passion or conquest, wander where they will,
Attend upon them still.

But now they drift on the still water,
Mysterious, beautiful;
Among what rushes will they build,
By what lake's edge or pool
Delight men's eyes when I awake some day
To find they have flown away?

W.B. Yeats

Not a poem for children or about childhood, 'The Wild Swans at Coole' nonetheless evokes powerful childhood memories for me, especially of my school and the remarkable teacher of drama and poetry who was an inspiration in my life. Born in October myself, I loved the autumn mood of the poem and the wonderfully detailed, visual descriptions of the 59 swans. The sense of loss, regret and underlying sadness in the poet's voice held a strong appeal too.

Gabrielle Cliff Hodges

1993 -

SILVER

Slowly, silently, now the moon
Walks the night in her silver shoon;
This way, and that, she peers, and sees
Silver fruit upon silver trees;
One by one the casements catch
Her beams beneath the silvery thatch;
Couched in his kennel, like a log,
With paws of silver sleeps the dog;
From their shadowy cote the white breasts peep
Of doves in a silver-feathered sleep;
A harvest mouse goes scampering by,
With silver claws, and silver eye;
And moveless fish in the water gleam,
By silver reeds in a silver stream.

Walter de la Mare

'Silver' is the first poem I remember having to learn by heart at primary school. I liked it, although the word 'shoon' was always rather perplexing. Once we had learnt it we took it in turns to recite it to the teacher. It was an awkward poem for anyone in the class who had temporarily lost their front teeth.

Helen Bunton

1955 - 1981

I REMEMBER, I REMEMBER

I remember, I remember,
The house where I was born,
The little window where the sun
Came peeping in at morn;
He never came a wink too soon,
Nor brought too long a day,
But now, I often wish the night
Had borne my breath away!

I remember, I remember,
The roses, red and white,
The violets, and the lily-cups,
Those flowers made of light!
The lilacs where the robin built,
And where my brother set
The laburnum on his birthday, -
The tree is living yet!

I remember, I remember,
Where I was used to swing,
And thought the air must rush as fresh
To swallows on the wing;
My spirit flew in feathers then,
That is so heavy now,
And summer pools could hardly cool
The fever on my brow!

I remember, I remember,
The fir trees dark and high;
I used to think their slender tops
Were close against the sky:
It was a childish ignorance,
But now 'tis little joy
To know I'm farther off from heav'n
Than when I was a boy.

Thomas Hood.

Although it doesn't exactly describe the house where I grew up, it is a picture of country tranquillity after the first world war. Why I chose it - sheer nostalgia!

Elizabeth Brewer

1966 - 1988

THE DAFFODILS

I wandered lonely as a cloud
That floats on high o'er vales and hills,
When all at once I saw a crowd,
A host, of golden daffodils;
Beside the lake, beneath the trees,
Fluttering and dancing in the breeze.

Continuous as the stars that shine
And twinkle on the milky way,
They stretched in never-ending line
Along the margin of a bay:
Ten thousand saw I at a glance,
Tossing their heads in sprightly dance.

The waves beside them danced; but they
Out-did the sparkling waves in glee:
A poet could not but be gay,
In such a jocund company:
I gazed - and gazed - but little thought
What wealth the show to me had brought:

For oft, when on my couch I lie
In vacant or in pensive mood,
They flash upon that inward eye
Which is the bliss of solitude;
And then my heart with pleasure fills,
And dances with the daffodils.

William Wordsworth.

The poem I loved as a little girl was Wordsworth's 'Daffodils', because we had hundreds of daffodils in our garden in spring, and I felt at about the age of eight, that it perfectly expressed the essential quality of daffodils. It is the first poem I remember caring about, and I owe my love of English literature to that experience of poetry.

Tim Everton

1992 -

DURING WIND AND RAIN

They sing their dearest songs -
He, she, all of them - yea,
Treble and tenor and bass,
And one to play;
With the candles mooning each face....
Ah, no; the years O!
How the sick leaves reel down in throngs!

They clear the creeping moss -
Elders and juniors - aye,
Making the pathways neat
And the garden gay;
And they build a shady seat....
Ah, no; the years, the years;
See, the white storm-birds wing across!

They are blithely breakfasting all -
Men and maidens - yea,
Under the summer tree,
With a glimpse of the bay,
While pet fowl come to the knee....
Ah, no; the years O!
And the rotten rose is ript from the wall.

They change to a high new house,
He, she, all of them - aye,
Clocks and carpets and chairs
On the lawn all day,
And brightest things that are theirs....
Ah, no; the years, the years;
Down their carved names the rain-drop ploughs.

Thomas Hardy

During my time at secondary school I was a great Hardy enthusiast and read all his novels and poems. This poem had a particular appeal for me. Perhaps strangely for Hardy, it seemed to offer comfort at several levels. At one level it conveys the domestic comfort of family life; at another it projects the comfort that I have always gained from the transitory nature of the life of an individual and the realisation that one's own influence and responsibility are of infinitesimal significance in the overall scheme of things.

Malcolm Pointon

1969 - 1992

RAIN

There are holes in the sky
  Where the rain gets in
But they're ever so small
  That's why rain is thin.

Spike Milligan

It extends rationality. I used to quote this when we were driving in the car through rain, and the children on the back seat would laugh and join in.

Barbara Pointon

1963 - 1993

THE ICE CART

Perched on my city office-stool
I watched with envy while a cool
And lucky carter handled ice. . . .
And I was wandering in a trice
Far from the gray and grimy heat
Of that intolerable street
O'er sapphire berg and emerald floe
Beneath the still, cold ruby glow
Of everlasting Polar night,
Bewildered by the queer half-light,
Until I stumbled unawares
Upon a creek where big white bears
Plunged headlong down with flourished heels
And floundered after shining seals
Through shivering seas of blinding blue.
And, as I watched them, ere I knew,
I'd stripped and I was swimming, too,
Among the seal-pack, young and hale,
And thrusting on with threshing tail,
With twist and twirl and sudden leap
Through crackling ice and salty deep,
Diving and doubling with my kind
Until at last we left behind
Those big white blundering bulks of death,
And lay at length with panting breath
Upon a far untravelled floe,
Beneath a gentle drift of snow -
Snow drifting gently, fine and white
Out of the endless Polar night,
Falling and falling evermore
Upon that far untravelled shore
Till I was buried fathoms deep
Beneath that cold white drifting sleep -
Sleep drifting deep,
Deep drifting sleep. . . .

The carter cracked a sudden whip:
I clutched my stool with startled grip,
Awakening to the grimy heat
Of that intolerable street.

Wilfred Wilson Gibson

My reason for choosing this is that it was the first poem which brought home to me the importance of poetry being read aloud.
I was in the First Form at Grammar School, it was a very hot day, and our English teacher read this to us. We all literally nodded off ourselves, lulled by its rhythm (.. "floe on floe" .. etc.) and she got quieter and quieter. Then her voice cut through like the crack of the whip itself and I jumped out of my skin, along, I suspect, with most of the others in the class. I think this was my first awakening to the power of poetry.

John Hopkins

1988 -

HARRIET

Spring moved to summer - the rude cold rain
hurries the ambitious, flowers and youth;
our flash-tones crackle for an hour, and then
we too follow nature, imperceptibly
change our mouse-brown to white lion's mane,
thin white fading to a freckled, knuckled skull,
bronzed by decay, by many, many suns . . .
Child of ten, three quarters animal,
three years from Juliet, half Juliet,
already ripened for the night on stage -
beautiful petals, what shall we hope for,
knowing one choice not two is all you're given,
health beyond the measure, dangerous
to yourself, more dangerous to others?

Robert Lowell.

It seems to catch the pathos of the brevity of childhood, and the pathos of parents watching their children grow towards an uncertain future. There's also a lovely setting of it by Elliott Carter in his cycle 'In Sleep, In Thunder.'

David Bridges

1968 - 1990

He hath disgrac'd me and hind'red me half a million;
laughed at my losses,
mock'd at my gains,
scorned my nation,
thwarted my bargains,
cooled my friends,
heated my enemies.
And what's his reason?

I am a Jew.

Hath not a Jew eyes?
Hath not a Jew hands, organs, dimensions, senses, affections,
passions,
fed with the same food,
hurt with the same weapons,
subject to the same diseases,
healed by the same means,
warmed and cooled by the same winter and summer,
as a Christian is?

If you prick us, do we not bleed?
If you tickle us, do we not laugh?
If you poison us, do we not die?

And if you wrong us, shall we not revenge?

William Shakespeare
Merchant of Venice Act 3 Scene 1

I was born and brought up in Warwickshire within cycling distance of Shakespeare's birthplace and the Royal Shakespeare Theatre, or Shakespeare Memorial Theatre as it was then known. Throughout my secondary school days there were regular trips to the theatre (five shillings a time for a seat in the Gods, the return coach fare and a chance to meet the girls from the local high school). The annual school play, almost inevitably a Shakespearean production, was for me a highlight of the year, even if, as a thirteen year old in an all boys' school, this required me to play the part of Titania in A Midsummer Night's Dream.

The piece I have chosen is on the polemical side of poetry, but there is still something in the rhythm, and the passion of this piece, not to mention the point of its content, which sends a thrill up my spine, and that is part of what I expect poetry to do. A few years ago I would probably not have thought this an appropriate piece for children, but the work that teachers now do with Shakespeare in schools shows that there are few such limitations.

Jill Waterhouse

1974 - 1990

STEPPING OUT

I'm stepping out, don't mess about.
Don't tell me to be patient.
I've been wedded, enslaved, white washed, and saved,
But now, I'm liberated.
I've been patted, and moulded, and shaped, and scolded
And I learned real fast how to please 'em,
I 'Yessir'ed, and 'No Ma'am'ed,
I was cursed and damned,
And all for no good reason.
I've been put up, and I've been put down,
By folks who were black, white, yellow or brown,
Treated like I wasn't human, just a puppet, a token,
But I healed my hurts, 'cause for better or worse,
Black woman's got spirit that's never going to be broken.
Been labelled all my life,
Black, woman, mother and wife.
And their labels formed the bars of my prison,
But I've got to set free, this person who's me.
'Cause now I've got a vision,
Their myths and lies are dead,
Not heaped on my head,
And their history is all outdated,
Different sex, different skin, can't change what's within,
'Cause now, I'm liberated,
And I'm stepping out, don't mess about,
Don't tell me to be patient,
No ifs or buts.
I don't walk, I strut,
'Cause now, I'm liberated.

Maureen Watson
(an Aborigine poem)

This poem is to be shouted rather than whispered, a marching poem. Maureen Watson is one of many Australian Aboriginal poets who, as this millenium draws to a close, calls our attention to outdated historical interpretations and the dangers of labelling people. As an historian, I am interested in her expression of tension between bitterness and self-confidence.

Ian Shearman

1989 -

from TREBETHERICK

We used to picnic where the thrift
Grew deep and tufted to the edge;
We saw the yellow foam-flakes drift
In trembling sponges on the ledge
Below us, till the wind would lift
Them up the cliff and o'er the hedge.
Sand in the sandwiches, wasps in the tea,
Sun on the bathing-dresses heavy with the wet,
Squelch of the bladder-wrack waiting for the sea,
Fleas round the tamarisk, an early cigarette.

- -

But when a storm was at its height,
And feathery slate was black in rain,
And tamarisks were hung with light
And golden sand was brown again,
Spring tide and blizzard would unite
And sea came flooding up the lane.
Waves full of treasure then were roaring up the beach,
Ropes round our mackintoshes, waders warm and dry,
We waited for the wreckage to come swirling into reach,
Ralph, Vasey, Alastair, Biddy, John and I.

Then roller into roller curled
And thundered down the rocky bay,
And we were in a water-world
Of rain and blizzard, sea and spray,
And one against the other hurled
We struggled round to Greenaway.
Blesséd be St. Enodoc, blesséd be the wave,
Blesséd be the springy turf, we pray, pray to thee,
Ask for our children all the happy days you gave
To Ralph, Vasey, Alastair, Biddy, John and me.

John Betjeman

This poem captures the sense and whole being, of what for me has long been a very special place. He wrote this poem in the early 1940's and the magic of the area clearly has not changed.

Jean Rudduck

1994 -

WEATHERS

(i)

This is the weather the cuckoo likes,
  And so do I;
When showers betumble the chestnut spikes,
  And nestlings fly:
And the little brown nightingale bills his best,
And they sit outside at 'The Travellers' Rest',
And maids come forth sprig-muslin drest,
And citizens dream of the south and west,
  And so do I.

(ii)

This is the weather the shepherd shuns,
  And so do I;
When beeches drip in browns and duns,
  And thresh, and ply;
And hill-hid tides throb, throe on throe,
And meadow rivulets overflow,
And drops on gate-bars hang in a row,
And rooks in families homeward go,
  And so do I.

Thomas Hardy

Education at my small convent school was, organisationally, a haphazard and bewildering experience but there were many good moments. Two were about speaking in chorus: the rapid sequencing of French vowels (oo, oh, aw, ah: a, eh, ch, ee, and so on) - all of us with identical goldfish mouthings, and our enthusiastic chanting of 'Weathers'. Looking back, I realise how little - at 7 or 8 years old - I understood the words: 'bills his best', 'drip in browns and duns', 'tides throb, throe on throe', but it didn't seem to matter. What we liked, I think, was the communal energy of the rhythm and the simple assertiveness of the beginning and ending of the verses: 'And so do I'.

Helen Arnold

1964 -

THE LAKE ISLE OF INNISFREE

I will arise and go now, and go to Innisfree,
And a small cabin build there, of clay and wattles made:
Nine bean-rows will I have there, a hive for the honey-bee,
   And live alone in the bee-loud glade.

And I shall have some peace there, for peace comes dropping slow,
Dropping from the veils of the morning to where the cricket sings;
There midnight's all a glimmer, and noon a purple glow,
   And evening full of the linnet's wings.

I will arise and go now, for always night and day
I hear lake water lapping with low sounds by the shore;
While I stand on the roadway, or on the pavements grey,
   I hear it in the deep heart's core.

W.B. Yeats

This poem sings in my head at least once a day.

Lucy Pyatt

Sallie Purkis

1977 - 1991

THE LISTENERS

"Is there anybody there?" said the Traveller,
Knocking on the moonlit door;
And his horse in the silence champed the grasses
Of the forest's ferny floor;
And a bird flew up out of the turret,
Above the Traveller's head;
And he smote upon the door again a second time;
"Is there anybody there?" he said.
But no one descended to the Traveller;
No head from the leaf-fringed sill
Leaned over and looked into his grey eyes,
Where he stood perplexed and still.
But only a host of phantom listeners
That dwelt in the lone house then
Stood listening in the quiet of the moonlight
To that voice from the world of men:
Stood thronging the faint moonbeams on the dark stair,
That goes down to the empty hall,
Hearkening in an air stirred and shaken
By the lonely Traveller's call.
And he felt in his heart their strangeness,
Their stillness answering his cry,
While his horse moved, cropping the dark turf,
'Neath the starred and leafy sky;
For he suddenly smote on the door, even
Louder, and lifted his head:
"Tell them I came, and no one answered
That I kept my word," he said.
Never the least stir made the listeners,
Thought every word he spake
Fell echoing through the shadowiness of the still house
From the one man left awake:
Ay, they heard his foot upon the stirrup,
And the sound of iron on stone,
And how the silence surged softly backward,
When the plunging hoofs were gone.

Walter de la Mare

I loved this poem because it was a drama, a painting and a detective story all rolled in together. Elements of the language I still like as I read it today are the alliterative 'forest's ferny floor', the visual 'leafy-fringed sill' and the 'faint moonbeams on the stair'. I still wonder about the 'phantom listeners' - was anyone there? What was it all about?

Eve Bearne

1988 -

from THE HIGHWAYMAN

The wind was a torrent of darkness among the gusty trees,
The moon was a ghastly galleon tossed upon cloudy seas,
The road was a ribbon of moonlight over the purple moor,
And the highwayman came riding -
        Riding - riding -
The highwayman came riding, up to the old inn-door.
He'd a French cocked-hat on his forehead, a bunch of lace at his chin,
A coat of the claret velvet, and breeches of brown doeskin:
They fitted with never a wrinkle; his boots were up to the thigh!
And he rode with a jewelled twinkle,
        His pistol butts a-twinkle,
His rapier hilt a-twinkle, under the jewelled sky.

Over the cobbles he clattered and clashed in the dark inn-yard,
And he tapped with his whip on the shutters, but all was locked and barred:
He whistled a tune to the window; and who should be waiting there
But the landlord's black-eyed daughter,
        Bess, the landlord's daughter,
Plaiting a dark red love-knot into her long black hair.

And dark in the dark old inn-yard a stable-wicket creaked
Where Tim, the ostler, listened; his face was white and peaked,
His eyes were hollows of madness, his hair like moldy hay;
But he loved the landlord's daughter,
        The landlord's red-lipped daughter:
Dumb as a dog he listened, and he heard the robber say -

'One kiss, my bonny sweetheart, I'm after a prize tonight,
But I shall be back with the yellow gold before the morning light.
Yet if they press me sharply, and harry me through the day,
Then look for me by moonlight,
        Watch for me by moonlight:
I'll come to thee by moonlight, though Hell should bar the way.'

Alfred Noyes

Poetry was one of the most remarkable features of our (very ordinary) childhood. My mother used to sing to us and read and speak poetry so that my memories of early childhood are almost always coloured by verse. This one was a favourite - it's visual, romantic, subversive and wonderfully melodramatic and sentimental!

Tim Rowland

1979 -

MRS. MALONE

Mrs. Malone
Lived hard by a wood
All on her lonesome
As nobody should.
With her crust on a plate
And her pot on the coal
And none but herself
To converse with, poor soul.
In a shawl and a hood
She got sticks out-o'-door,
On a bit of old sacking
She slept on the floor,
And nobody, nobody
Asked how she fared
Or knew how she managed,
For nobody cared.
 Why make a pother
 About an old crone?
 What for should they bother
 With Mrs. Malone?

One Monday in winter
With snow on the ground
So thick that a footstep
Fell without sound,
She heard a faint frostbitten
Peck on the pane
And went to the window
To listen again.
There sat a cock-sparrow
Bedraggled and weak,
With half-open eyelid
And ice on his beak.
She threw up the sash
And she took the bird in,
And mumbled and fumbled it
Under her chin.
 'Ye're all of a smother,
 Ye're fair overblown!
 I've room fer another,'
 Said Mrs. Malone.

Come Tuesday while eating
Her dry morning slice
With the sparrow a-picking
('Ain't company nice!')
She heard on her doorpost
A curious scratch,
And there was a cat
With its claw on the latch.
It was hungry and thirsty
And thin as a lath,
It mewed and it mowed
On the slithery path.
She threw the door open
And warmed up some pap,
And huddled and cuddled it
In her old lap.
 'There, there, little brother,
 Ye poor skin-an'-bone,
 There's room fer another,'
 Said Mrs. Malone.

Come Wednesday while all of them
Crouched on the mat
With a crumb for the sparrow,
A sip for the cat,
There was wailing and whining
Outside in the wood,
And there sat a vixen
With six of her brood.
She was haggard and ragged
And worn to a shred,
And her half-dozen babies
Were only half-fed,
But Mrs. Malone, crying
'My! ain't they sweet!'
Happed them and lapped them
And gave them to eat.
 'You warm yerself, mother,
 Ye're cold as a stone!
 There's room fer another,'
 Said Mrs. Malone.

Come Thursday a donkey
Stepped in off the road
With sores on his withers
From bearing a load.
Come Friday when icicles
Pierced the white air
Down from the mountainside
Lumbered a bear.
For each she had something,
If little, to give -
'Lord knows, the poor critters
Must all of 'em live.'
She gave them her sacking,
Her hood and her shawl,
Her loaf and her teapot -
She gave them her all.
'What with one thing and t'other
Me fambily's grown,
And there's room fer another,'
Said Mrs. Malone.

Come Saturday evening
When time was to sup
Mrs. Malone
Had forgot to sit up.
The cat said *meeow*,
And the sparrow said *peep*,
The vixen, *she's sleeping*,
The bear, *let her sleep*.
On the back of the donkey
They bore her away,
Through trees and up mountains
Beyond night and day,
Till come Sunday morning
They brought her in state
Through the last cloudbank
As far as the Gate.
'Who is it,' asked Peter,
You have with you there?'
And donkey and sparrow,
Cat, vixen and bear
Exclaimed, 'Do you tell us
Up here she's unknown?
It's our mother, God bless us!
It's Mrs. Malone
Whose havings were few
And whose holding was small
And whose heart was so big
It had room for us all.'
Then Mrs. Malone
Of a sudden awoke,
She rubbed her two eyeballs
And anxiously spoke:
'Where am I, to goodness,
And what do I see?
My dears, let's turn back,
This ain't no place fer me!'
But Peter said, 'Mother
Go in to the Throne.
There's room for another
One, Mrs. Malone.'

Eleanor Farjeon

It's 1950, and this is a world contained in two rooms, where everything stands still for "Listen with Mother". I recall my mother reading "Mrs Malone" from a thin paperback. It is comfortable verse, secure and certain. For me it was, it is, about virtue in poverty, about the reward of generosity, in the end.

Julia Swindells

1989 -

THE LUMB BANK CHILDREN

Today we walk here where once the miller walked
Imprisoned in time
Confined for a week to the beauty that is now

In the valley the mist hardly ever lifts
the hands that hold that white blanket down
are children's hands, they say
and that wail that wanders nightly
on this December wind
is not a christmas carol
but children howling an ancient hunger
around the mill-house
a gaunt memory of a living graveyard

Last night, while a child's mangled memory
moaned under the misty white
a ghost walked from ancient India's cotton-fields
moved tall and stately through this lonely valley house
connecting

Last night, while wailing carols wandered
in the whitening cold
a figure walked through time and space
from a water-mill somewhere near a Caribbean
cane-field
searching

The restless ghost-child sighed, sucked a thumb,
turned over in her valley bed, and slept.
Early this morning, the mist lifted slowly
And the waterfall shouted a story louder than its voice.

Today we walked where once the miller walked
Released in time
Surrounded for a week by the quiet beauty that is now

Merle Collins

In making my choice for the anthology, I have vacillated between poetry that I have known and worked with for years, and that which is comparatively new to me, such as the work of the Caribbean poets. This poem by the Grenadian writer, Merle Collins, seemed to provide me with the answer. It draws both on a world that I know well - an atmospheric Northern English landscape - and on ideas with which I have only worked recently, about the ways in which other cultures and races perceive and write about the relationship to Britain and to English. By placing the Lumb Bank children alongside the haunting figures from ancient India and the Caribbean canefield, the poem reminds us that children, along with those figures from colonial history, have often been the victims of tyranny and oppression; but we can also take some comfort from the beauty of the scene today, and from the tenderness with which the ghost child is portrayed.

Jane Edden

1986 -

WHEN I DANCE

When I dance it isn't merely
That music absorbs my shyness,
My laughter settles in my eyes,
My swings of arms convert my frills
As timing tunes my feet with floor
As if I never just looked on.

It is that when I dance
I'm costumed in a rainbow mood,
I'm okay at any angle,
Outfit of drums crowds madness round,
Talking winds and plucked strings conspire,
Beat after beat warms me like sun.

It is that when I dance
O music expands my hearing
And it wants no mathematics,
It wants no thinking, no speaking,
It only wants all my feeling
In with animation of place.

When I dance it isn't merely
I shift bodyweight balances
As movement amasses my show,
I celebrate each dancer here,
No sleep invades me now at all
And I see how I am tireless.

When I dance it isn't merely
That surprises dictate movements,
Other rhythms move my rhythms,
I uncradle rocking-memory
And skipping, hopping and running
All mix movements I balance in.

It is that when I dance
I gather up all my senses
Well into hearing and feeling,
With body's flexible postures
Telling their poetry in movement
And I celebrate all rhythms.

James Berry

Not only do I understand the poet's affinity with the absorption of the medium of dance. I see he touches on how the dance holds the human being in its spell. I am reminded of the year I spent in Trinidad, when I saw at first hand the ability of a people to celebrate life through dance. To 'jump up' in Carnival, both with children I taught and with thousands of revellers on the streets of Port of Spain, was a privilege, and an experience I shall always remember with affection.

Christine Poulson

1990 -

THE LADY OF SHALOTT

PART III

A BOW-SHOT from her bower-eaves,
He rode between the barley-sheaves,
The sun came dazzling thro' the leaves,
And flamed upon the brazen greaves
Of bold Sir Lancelot.
A red-cross knight for ever kneel'd
To a Lady in his shield,
That sparkled on the yellow field,
Beside remote Shalott.

The gemmy bridle glitter'd free,
Like to some branch of stars we see
Hung in the golden Galaxy.
The bridle bells rang merrily
As he rode down to Camelot:
And from his blazon'd baldric slung
A mighty silver bugle hung,
And as he rode his armour rung,
Beside remote Shalott.

All in the blue unclouded weather
Thick-jewell'd shone the saddle-leather,
The helmet and the helmet-feather
Burn'd like one burning flame together,
As he rode down to Camelot.
As often thro' the purple night,
Below the starry clusters bright,
Some bearded meteor, trailing light,
Moves over still Shalott.

His broad clear brow in sunlight glow'd;
On burnish'd hooves his war-horse trode;
From underneath his helmet flow'd
His coal-black curls as on he rode,
As he rode down to Camelot.
From the bank and from the river
He flashes into the crystal mirror,
"Tirra lirra," by the river
Sang Sir Lancelot.

She left the web, she left the loom,
She made three paces thro' the room,
She saw the water-lily bloom,
She saw the helmet and the plume,
She look'd down to Camelot.
Out flew the web and floated wide;
The mirror crack'd from side to side;
"The curse is come upon me," cried
The Lady of Shalott.

Alfred Tennyson.

I've chosen this because the drama, mystery and romance of Tennyson's poem enthralled me. I liked the strong rhythm and the powerful images: it was easy to memorise and I knew it off by heart.

THE WAY THROUGH THE WOODS

They shut the road through the woods
Seventy years ago.
Weather and rain have undone it again,
And now you would never know
There was once a road through the woods
Before they planted the trees.

It is underneath the coppice and heath
And the thin anemones.
Only the keeper sees
That, where the ring-dove broods,
And the badgers roll at ease,
There was once a road through the woods.

Yet, if you enter the woods
Of a summer evening late,
When the night-air cools on the trout-ringed pools
Where the otter whistles his mate,
(They fear not men in the woods,
Because they see so few.)
You will hear the beat of a horse's feet,
And the swish of a skirt in the dew,
Steadily cantering through
The misty solitudes,
As though they perfectly knew
The old lost road through the woods . . . .
But there is no road through the woods.

Rudyard Kipling

Between the ages of eight and twelve years I remember having to learn many poems by heart. Most of them are lost to me now, but this one has always remained . . .

Lesley Hendy

1990 -

THE DESTRUCTION OF SENNACHERIB

The Assyrian came down like the wolf on the fold,
And his cohorts were gleaming in purple and gold;
And the sheen of their spears was like stars on the sea,
When the blue wave rolls nightly on deep Galilee.

Like the leaves of the forest when Summer is green,
That host with their banners at sunset were seen:
Like the leaves of the forest when Autumn hath blown,
That host on the morrow lay withered and strown.

For the Angel of Death spread his wings on the blast,
And breathed in the face of the foe as he passed;
And the eyes of the sleepers waxed deadly and chill,
And their hearts but once heaved, and for ever grew still.

And there lay the steed with his nostril all wide,
But through it there rolled not the breath of his pride:
And the foam of his gasping lay white on the turf,
And cold as the spray of the rock-beating surf.

And there lay the rider distorted and pale,
With the dew on his brow and the rust on his mail;
And the tents were all silent, the banners alone,
The lances unlifted, the trumpet unblown.

And the widows of Ashur are loud in their wail,
And the idols are broke in the temple of Baal;
And the might of the Gentile, unsmote by the word,
Hath melted like snow in the glance of the Lord!

Lord Byron

I remember this poem as a child because of its unusual (for me at the time) rhythm.

John A. Hammond

1965 -

OZYMANDIAS

I met a traveller from an antique land
Who said: Two vast and trunkless legs of stone
Stand in the desert.... Near them, on the sand,
Half sunk, a shattered visage lies, whose frown
And wrinkled lip, and sneer of cold command
Tell that its sculptor well those passions read
Which yet survive, stamped on these lifeless things,
The hand that mocked them, and the heart that fed;
And on the pedestal these words appear:
'My name is Ozymandias, king of kings:
Look on my works, ye Mighty, and despair!'
Nothing beside remains. Round the decay
Of that colossal wreck, boundless and bare
The lone and level sands stretch far away.

Percy Bysshe Shelley

At secondary school I had an English teacher called Mr Gillett. He introduced me to poetry over the two or three years that he taught my class. We had to record them in our books and illustrate them, as well as learn and recite them. I can still recall my illustration of 'Ozymandias'; it seemed to coincide with my awareness of great building feats like the pyramids.

Beth Hodges

Janet Scott

1989 -

SIMON THE CYRENIAN SPEAKS

He never spoke a word to me,
    And yet He called my name;
He never gave a sign to me,
    And yet I knew and came.

At first I said, "I will not bear
    His cross upon my back;
He only seeks to place it there
    Because my skin is black."

But He was dying for a dream,
    And He was very meek,
And in His eyes there shone a gleam
    Men journey far to seek.

It was Himself my pity bought;
    I did for Christ alone
What all of Rome could not have wrought
    With bruise of lash or stone.

Countee Cullen

My father had a book called 'Great Poems of the English Language' which I loved to dip into. His favourite was 'Abou Ben Adham' which I love too. But this one is one I found for myself - not, I think, intended for children, but it spoke to this child. You might note the early interest in religion, both multi-faith and multi-ethnic!

John Beck

1972 -

Quem pastores 8 8 8.7

German Mediaeval Melody

SON OF MAN

Jesus, good above all other,
gentle child of gentle mother,
in a stable born our brother,
  give us grace to persevere.

Jesus, cradled in a manger,
for us facing every danger,
living as a homeless stranger,
  make we thee our King most dear.

Jesus, for thy people dying,
risen Master, death defying,
Lord in heaven, thy grace supplying,
  keep us to thy presence near.

Jesus, who our sorrows bearest,
all our thoughts and hopes thous sharest,
thou to man the truth declarest;
  help us all thy truth to hear.

Lord, in all our doings guide us;
pride and hate shall ne'er divide us;
we'll go on with thee beside us,
  and with joy we'll persevere.

Pearcy Dearmer (1867-1936)
partly based on J.M. Neale (1818-66)

For some reason, this combination of simple melody and deceptively simple words is particularly evocative of a certain stage of my childhood.

Brigid Smith

1989 -

ABOU BEN ADHEM

ABOU BEN ADHEM (may his tribe increase!)
Awoke one night from a deep dream of peace,
And saw, within the moonlight in his room,
Making it rich, and like a lily in bloom,
An angel writing in a book of gold:-
Exceeding peace had made Ben Adhem bold,
And to the presence in the room he said,
'What writest thou?' - The vision raised its head,
And with a look made of all sweet accord,
Answered, 'The names of those who love the Lord.'
'And is mine one?' said Abou. 'Nay, not so,'
Replied the angel. Abou spoke more low,
But cheerly still; and said, 'I pray thee, then
Write me as one that loves his fellow men.'
The angel wrote, and vanished. The next night
It came again with a great wakening light,
And showed the names whom love of God had blest,
And lo! Ben Adhem's name led all the rest.

James Leigh Hunt

I had this poem in an Arthur Mee Golden Treasury Collection which was given to me as a Christmas present. I loved its resounding lines and cadences, reading it made my back prickle. I gave frequent renderings to a (largely bored) audience of dolls and teddy bears experiencing difficulties only in maintaining a balance between holding this very large, heavy green book and the need to throw my arms around at the exciting bits!

John Murrell

1968 - 1992

MORITURI SALUTAMUS

Is it too late? Ah, nothing is too late
Till the tired heart shall cease to palpitate.
Cato learned Greek at eighty; Sophocles
Wrote his grand Oedipus, and Simonides
Bore off the prize of verse from his compeers,
When each had numbered more than forescore years.
And Theophrastus at forescore and ten
Had but begun his Characters of Men.
Chaucer at Woodstock with the nightingales
At sixty wrote the Canterbury Tales;
Goethe at Weimar, toiling to the last,
Completed Faust when eighty years were past.

What then? Shall we sit idly down and say
The night hath come; it is no longer day?
The night hath not yet come; we are not quite
Cut off from labour by the failing light;
Something remains for us to do or dare;

For age is opportunity no less
Than youth itself, though in another dress,
And as the evening twilight fades away
The sky is filled with stars, invisible by day.

Henry Wadsworth Longfellow

In 1992, I had the honour of saying farewell on behalf of a group of Homerton colleagues who between them had amassed nearly three hundred years of service to the college. Many were making that strategic withdrawal known as premature retirement, and I looked for some way of expressing the strong feeling in the group that this was not the marking of an end, but of a new, and potentially creative change of perspective. I found the answer in the work of Longfellow, who on the fiftieth anniversary of the graduation of his university class, read a specially composed poem to which he gave the title 'Morituri Salutamus'. This salute of those about to die, given by gladiators to Caesar in the Roman arena, unpromising perhaps as a source of hope for the future, is my chosen poem.

Afterword :

'For, long ago, the truth to say,
She has grown up and gone away,
And it is but a child of air
That lingers in the garden there.'

Acknowledgements

I should like to thank the Principal, Homerton Publications Group and the Centenary Appeal Committee for supporting this endeavour. I am grateful to the following students for illustrating the poems : Elizabeth Connor, Natale Cremona, Gillian Curry, Helen Gomez-Reino, Beth Hodges, Jacqueline Kirk, Kate Millner and Suzanna Walker. Lucy Pyatt requires a special mention for providing the cover illustration as well as several others. Finally, I should like to express my warmest thanks to Alan Russell for the painstaking work he put into preparing the manuscript. Without him there would not have been a book.

Morag Styles

N.B. The date(s) underneath each tutor's name indicates when the person began work at Homerton and, in some cases, when they left.

We should like to thank the following people for permission to print poems:

- *Penguin Group for permission to print 'Headmaster's Hymn' by Allan Ahlberg from Please, Mrs Butler, copyright © Allan Ahlberg, 1983. First published by Viking Kestrel and available in Puffin Books;*
- *James Berry & Hamish Hamilton for quoting 'When I Dance' from When I Dance;*
- *Charles Causley for 'School at Four O'Clock' reprinted by kind permission of the author, Charles Causley: Collected Poems, 1992 (Macmillan);*
- *Merle Collins and Virago Press for permission to quote 'The Lumb Bank Children' from Rotten Pomerack;*
- *Trustees for the E.E. Cummings Trust for 'maggie and millie and mollie and may' (Copyright © 1984), reproduced with the permission of W.W. Norton and Company;*
- *Random House U.K. Ltd. for permission to quote 'Silver' and 'The Listeners' by Walter de la Mare;*
- *David Higham Associates for 'Mrs Malone' by Eleanor Farjeon from Silver, Sand and Snow published by Michael Joseph, reprinted by permission of David Higham Associates;*
- *'A Boy's Head' reprinted by permission of Bloodaxe Books Ltd. from: Miroslav Holub: Poems Before & After: Collected English Translations (Bloodaxe 1990);*
- *Ted Hughes and Faber & Faber for 'Roger the Dog' from What Is The Truth? 1984, reprinted by kind permission of the author;*
- *Roger McGough for 'First Day at School' from In the Glassroom, © 1976 (Jonathan Cape Ltd.);*
- *The Society of Authors as the literary representative of the Estate of John Masefield for permission to quote 'Sea Fever' and 'Cargoes' by John Masefield;*
- *Spike Milligan Productions Ltd. & Norma Farnes for 'Rain';*
- *Methuen Children's Books for permission to quote 'Market Square', 'The Three Foxes' and 'Before Tea' by A.A. Milne from When We Were Very Young;*
- *John Murray (Publishers) Ltd for 'The Highwayman' by Alfred Noyes and 'Trebetherick by John Betjeman;*
- *Michael Rosen for 'Don't' from Don't Put Mustard in the Custard, Andre Deutsch, 1985;*
- *James MacGibbon (executor) for 'Fafnir and the Knights' from The Collected Poems of Stevie Smith (Penguin 20th Century Classics);*
- *Faber and Faber Ltd. for permission to quote 'Harriet' by Robert Lowell in Selected Poems: Robert Lowell and 'Prayer before Birth' by Louis MacNeice in Collected Poems of Louis MacNeice, edited by E.R. Dodds.*
- *Anne and Ian Serraillier for kind permission to reprint 'The Rescue' by Ian Serraillier;*

The editor has made every effort to contact all copyright holders. If any omission has occurred, we would be grateful to hear from copyright holders, so that we can put it right.

Index

Index